My Colorado

A funny play on words with accurate Colorado facts.
What a great combination!

Carolyn G. - Ann's Hallmark, Fort Collins

An absolute must for every bathroom!

Peter S. - Maria's Bookshop, Durango

Love the bookmarks. So cool!

Daiva C. - Between the Covers Bookstore, Telluride

Humorous and informative. I like that!

Kara - Booklovers Bookstore, Fort Collins

Your fun and funny roadmap to Colorado.

Tim G. - Denver

My Colorado

By Ilan Shamir

Illustrations: Dale Crawford

Thanks to Dale Crawford for his great illustrative talent and delightful attitude; John Cole for book consultation, layout and production; Deanna Estes for colorizing Dale's cover illustrations, cover layout, and type selection. Much appreciation to the great team at Your True Nature especially Kim Baca, Allison Rittner, Jacque Haines and Patti Slade for fabulous ideas and editing; and to fellow NSA speaker and funny guy, Tim Gard, for bouncing ideas around with me. And, a big thanks to the people and beauty of Colorado.

ISBN: 9 781930 175280

Advice From™
is a trademark of Your True Nature, Inc.

Box 272309
Fort Collins, CO 80527
www.YourTrueNature.com
branch@yourtruenature.com

We plant twenty seedling trees
for each 500 books printed of *My Colorado*.
www.ReplantTrees.org

Printed in Canada to support our northern neighbors.

100% REPLANTED

Your True Nature®
Set it free!

I couldn't help thinking . . . "Life has gotten way too serious." Who better than me, a transplanted Texan, to polish a few shiny nuggets of colorful Colorado? It all started whizzing along I-70 towards Denver in my little green Toyota Prius with my luggage carrier and mountain bike on top. As I approached the Winter Park exit, traffic began to slow way down. OMG! Caught in Sunday afternoon highway crawl! What was I thinking? My positive psychology approach to life kicked in as I took a big breath, let go of the stress, and plastered a big smile on my lips. After all, this is the amazing state of Colorado. No worries.

With an abundant amount of highway time, ideas for this book came pouring out of me. With one hand on the wheel and the other grabbing a pen, I scrawled and crawled down the road at five mph. By the time traffic let up, two hours later, I had most of the funny punny material scribbled on miscellaneous scraps of paper for MY Colorado. Laugh, enjoy, and have fun — after all, it's **OUR** Colorado!

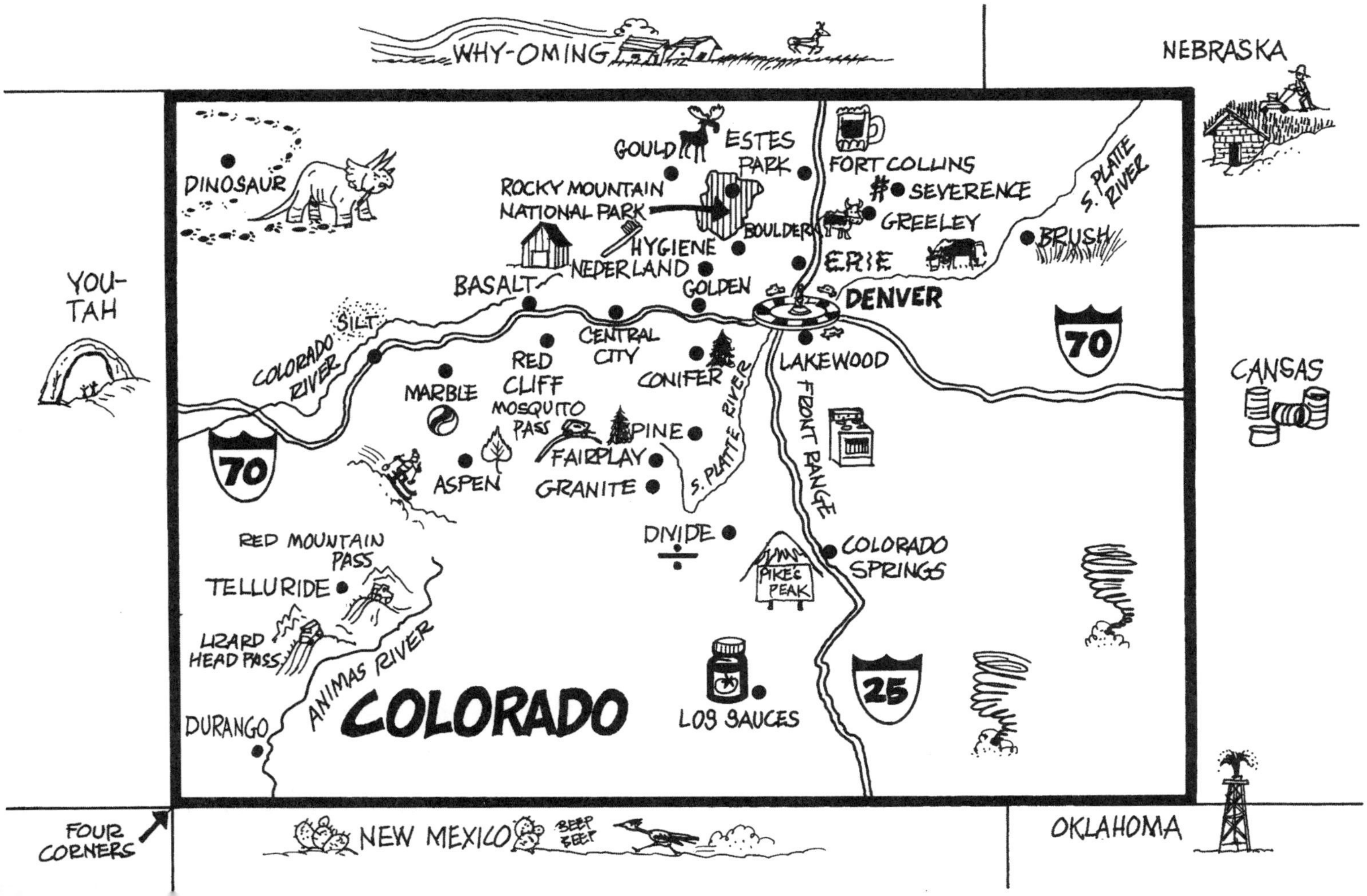
WHY-OMING
NEBRASKA
YOU-TAH
CANSAS
OKLAHOMA
NEW MEXICO
BEEP BEEP
FOUR CORNERS
DINOSAUR
GOULD
ESTES PARK
FORT COLLINS
SEVERENCE
GREELEY
ROCKY MOUNTAIN NATIONAL PARK
BOULDER
HYGIENE
NEDERLAND
ERIE
BRUSH
S. PLATTE RIVER
BASALT
GOLDEN
DENVER
SILT
COLORADO RIVER
CENTRAL CITY
RED CLIFF
MARBLE
CONIFER
LAKEWOOD
70
MOSQUITO PASS
PINE
S. PLATTE RIVER
FRONT RANGE
FAIRPLAY
ASPEN
GRANITE
DIVIDE
RED MOUNTAIN PASS
COLORADO SPRINGS
PIKES PEAK
TELLURIDE
LIZARD HEAD PASS
ANIMAS RIVER
25
COLORADO
LOS SAUCES
DURANGO

Is it always green in Evergreen?
Is there gold in Golden?

. . . Is it really
erie in Erie?
Do people
always
play fair
in Fairplay?

In Colorado, we're big on . . .

Recycling!

Did you know that Colorado has a front range?

. . . Maybe that's why so many people put their work on the back burner!

In the town of Estes Park there's
a whole new meaning to . . .

. . . the Elks Club!

The Spanish were the first
to call it Colorado . . .

. . . Good thing they didn't look at the blue rivers, we'd be called Colobluedo!

Denver is best known for
the Broncos, the Rockies,
and you guessed it . . .

... the Denver Omelet.

Colorado is one of the hardest places to live . . .

. . . You have
a choice
between
Boulder,
Basalt,
Granite,
Redstone,
Marble . . .

Coloradoans definitely know the meaning of . . .

. . . higher education.

The town of Dinosaur is worth visiting . . .

. . . Everyone there works really hard to make a good impression.

A lot of people go out on a limb
to live in . . .

. . . Conifer,
Aspen,
EverGREEN,
Pinecliffe,
Cherry Hills,
LakeWOOD,
EngleWOOD . . .

In Colorado, people are totally **WILD** . . .

. . . about the flowers!

If you're thinking of relocating to Colorado,
we highly suggest you visit the town of Silt . . .

. . . We've heard it's a very nice place to settle!

Sometimes, it's really hard to shed old relatives! . . .

. . . But the town of Nederland sure seems to have figured it out!

The Flatirons in Boulder are quite a sight! . . .

. . . People there are really pressed for time.

The Gold Rush started in 1859
near Central City . . .

. . . and happens again every fall.

Colorado has great visitor centers . . .

. . . You won't want to moose the one near Gould.

California has Los Angeles,
New Mexico has Los Alamos . . .

. . . In Colorado,
we have
Los Sauces!

With a name like Fort Collins, you'd
sure think they have a FORT somewhere . . .

. . . Not true! But anyway, things there are really hoppin'.

Water rights out here in the West . . .

. . . are often
a HOT topic.

People in Colorado are reel-ly . . .

. . . hooked
on getting
a good meal.

We're not saying there's nothing to do
North of here in Why-oming . . .

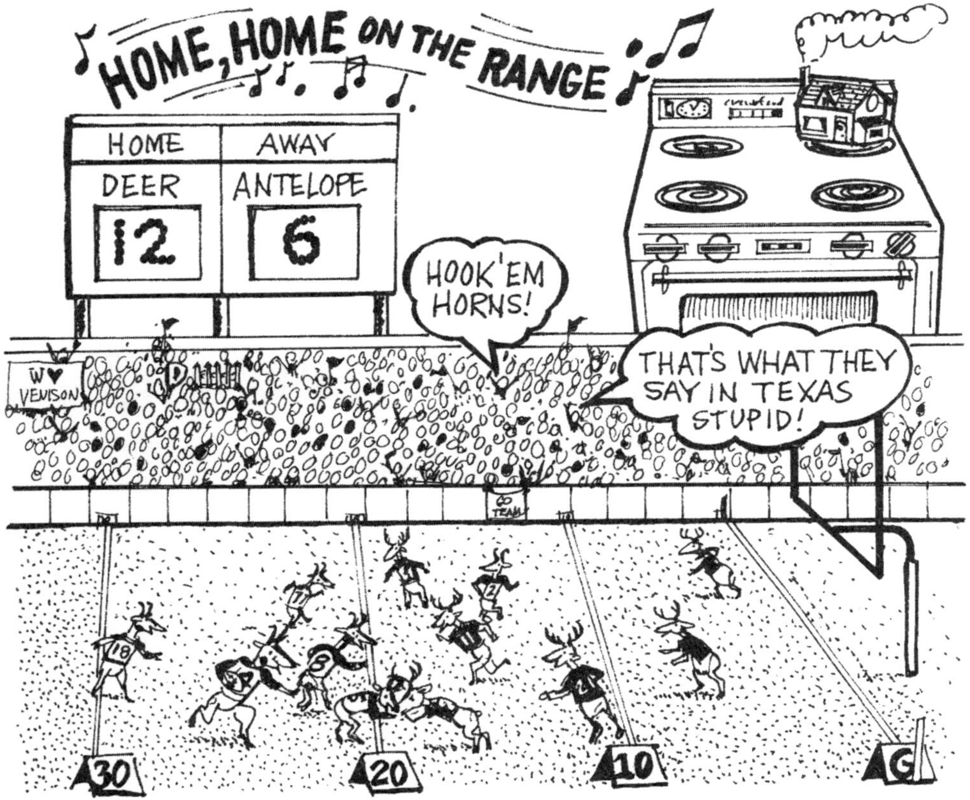

. . . but
their favorite
pastime is
watching the
deer and the
antelope play.

In Colorado, the land used to be UNDERwater,
the kids want to be UNDERstood . . .

. . . and the teachers are UNDERpaid!

Contrary to popular myth, we do have cloudy days in Colorado . . .

. . . Thursday
June 4, 1892 . . .
Saturday
April 6, 1907 . . .
Monday
September 14,
1964 . . .

We're not saying it's hard to find
city names in Colorado . . .

. . . but have you
ever been
to the town
of Brush?

In Colorado, most people are going . . .

. . . downhill fast!

One of the tallest mountains in Colorado is 14,259 ft. and is called Longs Peak . . .

. . . named after the fact that it's a very LONG way to the top!

People here are always hungry to get outside . . .

. . . There's the north FORK of the South Platte, the east FORK of the south FORK of the Crystal, the first FORK of the Piedra, the west FORK of the the San Juan, the north FORK of the Big Thompson. . . .

Do you know the difference between Greeley and Yogurt? . . .

THE SMELL OF MONEY
$ BANK $
ACME MOO-VERS
ALL BEEF HOTDOGS
AIR CONDITIONING
COME IN
THE FEEDLOT
GOOD FOOD
SMILIN' BULL'S
BBQ
THE WIND SURE IS BLOWING THE WRONG WAYTODAY!
HOLY COW!
YOGURT
NET. WT. 4 OZ.
THE CITY OF
GREELEY
POP. 84,000 HUMANS
195,000 COWS

. . . Culture!

Colorado has a town named Divide . . .

. . . Wonder if they can add as well?

Football is BIG in Colorado . . .

. . . there's a name for every PASS.

You won't want to miss one of the cleanest towns in Colorado . . .

JOB SECURITY!
.......SWEET!
HYGIENE STREET SWEEPER
ACE CLEANERS
open
CLEAN SWEEP
CARPET CLEANERS
BRUSH
BROOMFIELD
LET'S GO TO BRUSH FOR THE WEEKEND!
I'D RATHER GO TO BROOMFIELD!
COTTON WOOD TREE
CITY PARK
CLEANEST TOWN AROUND
HYGIENE
CITY LIMITS
WASH UP HERE
SCRUB! SCRUB! SCRUB!
SCRUB OAK
WOLF A-DUB-DUB!

. . . Hygiene.

Year after year, property values keep going . . .

OH NO, NOT ANOTHER BALLOON PAYMENT!
VISTA ACRES
HIGH VIEW ESTATES
JUST A LITTLE HIGHER!
WE'RE ALMOST THERE!

. . . up, Up, UP!

Did you know there's a town called
Colorado SPRINGS? . . .

. . . We've heard the place is kind of jumpy!

One thing's for sure . . .

. . . there's a heck of a lot of upward mobility in Colorado!

Folks in Colorado know everything there is to know about . . .

. . . streaming video.

In the fall, you sure don't want to miss the . . .

. . . Aspen quaking and the elk bugling.

The runoff starts in spring . . .

. . . and never seems to slow down.

There's no better place in Colorado
to get laid off . . .

. . . than
Severance.

Radium Hot Springs is very unique . . .

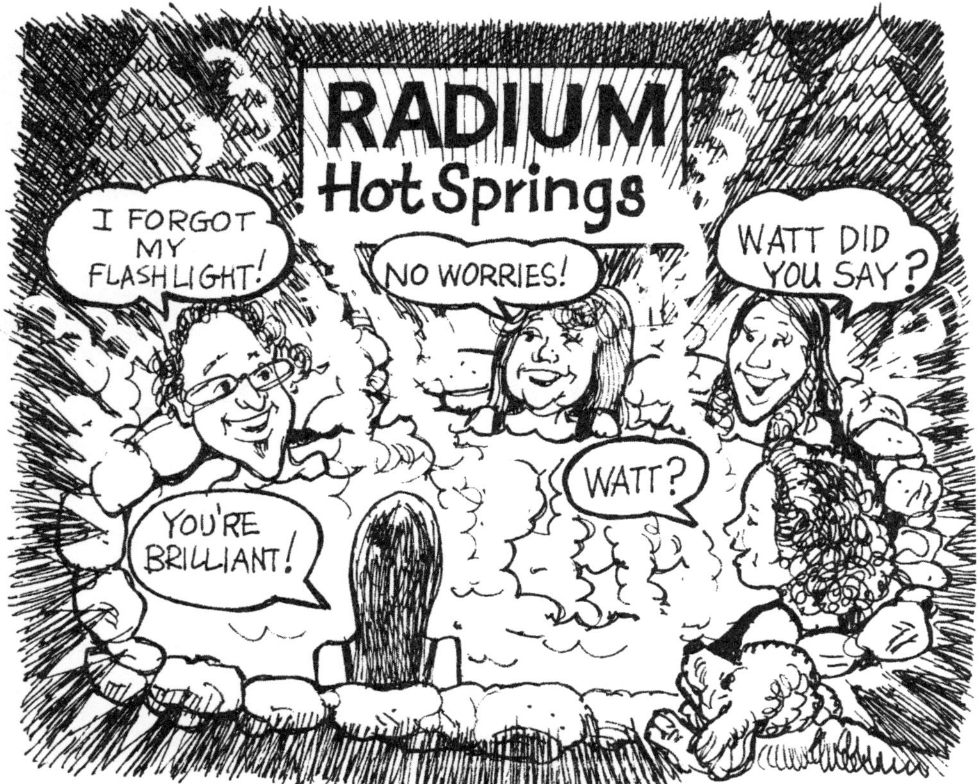

. . . The people that go there are all very bright and the place always gets glowing reviews!

We have five kinds of gambling in Colorado . . .

. . . I-25,
I-70,
I-76,
Hwy 285,
and
E-470!

The End!

The author
Ilan Shamir

Ilan saw his first snow on top of Pikes Peak, just west of Colorado Springs at the age of seven, during his family vacation from Texas. In his uncontrolled excitement to touch the frozen white stuff, he nearly slid down a deceptively steep snowfield, possibly to never be seen again. His quick thinking parents, in fear of losing their dependent tax deduction, rescued this adventuresome child, allowing him to grow up and share his worldly true nature.

Never losing his thirst for exploration, he has completed many adventures, including a 40-day solo trek across remote Iceland and a 25-day Swiss Alps jouney. Traveling to many exotic places has been one of Ilan's lifetime passions. He's spent many hours backpacking most of the beautiful wildernesses of Colorado. Ilan has lived in Boulder, Gold Hill, Fort Collins, Ridgway, and Durango.

After starting his successful career for 7UP during the wildly successful Uncola campaign and Willy Wonka candy bars in the early 1970's, Ilan gave up promoting sugar and devoted himself to giving voice to nature's many treasures. Ilan is well known as the "Advice Guy." He and his company, Your True Nature, continuously produce ideas and products for its popular Advice from Nature bookmarks, postcards, journals, T-shirts, and other products found in national parks and thousands of locations around the U.S.A., Australia, Canada, and other countries.

The illustrator

Dale Crawford

Dale escaped the holds of New York City on a freight train heading west. Sketching fellow travelers provided much appreciated sustenance. His humble career started in a shoe factory in Ohio, cheese factory in Wisconsin, small farmer in Iowa, before landing in Colorado to share his artistic talents as a book illustrator, graphics and caricature artist. Dale has illustrated more than 25 books including: *Strange But True Colorado* and *$10 Horse, $40 Saddle*. Dale lives in Fort Collins with his wife Fran and can be reached at bucksspurr@hotmail.com. Visit his website at CrawfordFineArt.com.

Fun Travel Notes: